D1264528

THE MOST IMPORTANT THING
I KNOW™

About Love

ALSO BY LORNE A. ADRAIN

THE MOST IMPORTANT THING I KNOW

THE MOST IMPORTANT THING I KNOW™
ABOUT THE SPIRIT OF SPORT

THE MOST IMPORTANT THING I KNOW™

About Love

INSPIRING MESSAGES FROM EMINENT
WRITERS, POETS, MUSICIANS,
THINKERS, AND OTHERS

COMPILED BY LORNE A. ADRAIN

William Morrow
An Imprint of HarperCollinsPublishers

Ruby Bridges-Hall stationery on page 87:
Printed by permission of the Norman Rockwell Family Trust
Copyright © 1964 by the Norman Rockwell Family Trust.

Copyright © 2000 by Lorne A. Adrain

All rights reserved. No part of this book may be reproduced or utilized in any form
or by any means, electronic or mechanical, including photocopying, recording, or by
any information storage or retrieval system, without permission in writing from the
Publisher. Inquiries should be addressed to Permissions Department, William Morrow
and Company, Inc., 1350 Avenue of the Americas, New York, N.Y. 10019.

It is the policy of William Morrow and Company, Inc., and its imprints and affiliates,
recognizing the importance of preserving what has been written, to print the books
we publish on acid-free paper, and we exert our best efforts to that end.

Library of Congress Cataloging-in-Publication Data

The most important thing I know about love : inspiring messages from eminent writers,
poets, musicians, thinkers, and others / compiled by Lorne A. Adrain—1st ed.
p. cm.
ISBN 0-688-16401-3
1. Love—Quotations, maxims, etc. I. Adrain, Lorne A.

PN6084.L6 M67 2000
302.3—dc21
99-047934

BOOK DESIGN BY JOANN METSCH

Printed in the United States of America

First Edition

1 2 3 4 5 6 7 8 9 10

www.williammorrow.com

For Ann
whose love helps light my way

LIST OF CONTRIBUTORS

ACKNOWLEDGMENTS

Thank you for buying this book. Your purchase will help support charities that help needy children to feel loved and happy and hopeful.

Thanks to the generous contributors to this project, those who risked thoughts often not shared in the interest of all of us learning something new. And a special thanks to Dr. Bernie Siegel, whose thoughtful foreword to this book reflects his generous spirit and kind assistance on the project.

Thanks to my family and friends for encouragement and inspiration, and especially to Ann Hood, who helped a simple compiler tell his story.

Thanks to my editor, Michelle Shinseki of William Morrow and Company, who believed in us and went to bat for us when even we wondered if this would come together. To Caroline Carney, whose unending confidence and great ideas helped us to believe in ourselves. To Vince Agliata, my assistant on this project, without whose making it happen, it would not have. To Jessi Hempel, whose cheerful and loving spirit is clearly reflected in the biographies of our contributors.

And to all those who have inspired me and helped me with this project in other ways—identifying people with great stories, finding people, getting people to respond, or inspiring dreams of what could be: Sue Aldrich, Bonnie Bacon, Lorraine Bandoni, Amy Barlow, Barbara Bejoian, Larry Berman, Laurie Beurman, Dick Butler, Bob Carothers, Karen Cummings, Hillary Day, Debbie Denenberg, Jennifer Devitt, Fred Dolan, David Filippone, Sam Grabelle, Ward Grant, Andrew Gold, Laura Haas, Ned Handy, Barbara Hagler, Linda Andrews Kendz, Franmarie Kennedy, Audrey Jones, Candace Lightner, Elaine MacLaughlin, Jean Main, Russ Marchand, Clara Mathieu, Alexandra Morehouse McReynolds, Sylvia Moore, Tracey Minkin, Michaela Prescott, Carol Culshaw Prince, Lee Ray, Brock Reeve, Shannon Russell, Carolyn Ryan, Rebecca Spencer, Jonathan Stone, Marilyn Suey, Bobbie-Jean Taylor, Danielle Thibeault, Newell Thomas, Kimberly Till, Angel Venable, Jennifer Wheeler, Carmen Westwater, and Richard Wurman.

The most important thing I know about love I learned from a personal experience with amnesia. A few years ago my ladder broke and I fell off the roof of our house, hitting my head on the pavement. I awakened to a beautiful lady bending over me saying, "Honey, are you all right?"

"Why are you calling me 'Honey'?" I asked.

"I'm your wife," she replied.

From the blow to my head, I developed amnesia, and it improved my marriage and family life immensely. 1 had no memories of the preceding day and had nothing to be upset or troubled over. All my problems started when I regained my memory. Then I had to seek therapy and marriage counseling. The counselor said, "1 am going to save you time and money by giving you something to read. Experience what is written here, and you will have all the benefits of amnesia and more."

I took what she handed me and read about something that is patient and kind, not jealous or boastful, not arrogant or rude, not irritable or resentful; that does not rejoice at wrong, but rejoices in the right, bears all things, believes all things, hopes all things, endures all things, and never ends. So faith, hope, and love abide, but the greatest of these is what the therapist recommended, love. What the therapist gave me to read was Corinthians 1:13, which showed me that love could give my life far more peace and joy than amnesia could ever provide.

When you understand the power of love, you understand statements like "Love is blind," "Kill 'em with kindness," "Love thine enemies," "Love is all you need," and "What the world needs now is love sweet love, that's the only thing that there's just too little of."

The power of love amazes me. It is blind to faults and obliterates enemies. I have seen its effect on families when one family member chooses to love the others despite past abuse. When the lover neglects to express love one day, the other, who until then has said nothing in response to "I love you," says, "You forgot something."

"What did I forget?"

"You forgot to say I love you."

Then come the tears and healing.

In *The Grand Inquisitor,* Dostoyevsky describes a Christ-like prisoner who is about to be burned at the stake, and the jailor is describing what tortures are planned for the prisoner the following day. When he is done, the prisoner doesn't scream back at him, as the jailor had expected. The prisoner walks over and kisses the jailor gently on his aged lips. At that point, the jailor opens the prison door and tells him to go. The power of love is awesome, especially when people have never experienced it. I make one exception to when to choose to stay and love. If your health or life are threatened, it may be best to remove yourself from the situation and love from a distance. Even then it can change the people loved.

We all need love to survive. Studies show that those who feel loved by their parents have one fourth the serious illness rate as adults. Studies on touch show similar effects on health and growth. Self-esteem and self-love lead to healthy behavior; their absence leads to self-destruction. It is hard to be an ugly duckling, feel lovable, and care for yourself. That is why we say, "Love thy neighbor as thyself." If you do not love yourself, your neighbor isn't going to experience your love either.

Being born an ugly duckling due to birth trauma, I know what the love and touch of a grandmother can do. She was capable of true unconditional love, and that love benefits the giver and receiver. My mother describes my appearance at birth as that of a purple melon. I was her first child, and she didn't know what to do with an infant she couldn't show anyone. My grandmother took me, anointed my head with oil, and, to quote my mother, "pushed everything back to where it belonged." Imagine how I felt being anointed and massaged several times a day by loving hands.

When you rescue a wounded animal, restore it to health, and release it again, how do you feel? That is a feeling that can't be described, and it doesn't require a thank-you call or card from the living thing you have given your love to. Love is a feeling and a phenomenon. It alters our sense of the passage of time, and keeps us from aging and free from pain and disease.

Just as this book is a collection of thoughts on love, let me share with you the insights and comments of some special people about love. Anthropologist Ashley Montagu has written a great deal about love. He gave me the most important advice I have ever received about love. When I asked him how I could be a more loving human being, he said, "Behave as if you are a loving human being."

What he helped me to understand is what every actor and athlete knows: You have to rehearse and practice to become good at something. So start behaving as if you are a lover and you, your life, and the people you love will all be changed. So choose a role model to emulate; it will help you to become a lover. I use Don Quixote and Lassie. Love now and reap the rewards for yourself and all those you meet. Remember, Don Quixote changed a prostitute and barmaid named Aldonza into the beautiful Dulcinea by his love. She tells him to stop tormenting her with tenderness, but he persists and she comes to love herself through his love for her.

Feel free to choose your way of giving love to the world, but remember, we are here to serve, not to be served. Love freely given is the greatest gift that we can bestow. I have visited the Garden of Eden and seen how boring it is when no choices or free will are available.

Ashley Montagu lists these qualities of love and says there are few lovers because we have been miseducated out of the capacity to be lovers, and trained to keep our eye on egotistical goals and self-gain rather than on altruism and love of our fellow man.

Love implies the possession of deep involvement in another, and to love another means to communicate that feeling of involvement to her.

Love is unconditional. It makes no bargains and trades with anyone for anything.

Love is supportive.

Love is firm.

Love is most needed by the human organism from the moment of birth.

Love is reciprocal in its effects, and is as beneficial to the giver as to the recipient.

Love is creative.

Love enlarges the capacities of those who are loved.

Love continually elicits, by encouragement, the nascent capabilities of the loved one.

Love is tender.

Love is joyful.

Love is fearless.

Love enables the person to treat life like an art.

Love as an attitude of mind and as a form of behavior is adaptively the best and most efficient of all adjustive processes in enabling the human being to adapt himself to his environment.

For the person and the species, love is the form of behavior having the highest survival value. Healer Emmet Fox said, "There is no difficulty that enough love will not conquer; no disease that enough love will not heal; no door that enough love will not open; no gulf that enough love will not bridge; no wall that enough love will not throw down; no sin that enough love will not redeem.

"It makes no difference how deeply seated may be the trouble, how hopeless the outlook, how muddled the tangle, how great the mistake; a sufficient realization of love will dissolve it all. If only you could love enough you would be the happiest and most powerful being in the world."

From philosopher Pierre Teilhard de Chardin: "Someday after we have harnessed the winds, the waves, the tides and gravity we shall harness for God the energies of love; and then for the second time in the history of the world man will have discovered fire."

If we could accomplish this love toward one another, the Messiah will appear and he'll be one day too late. Remember to be the mirror that reflects love back to all living things. Then the ugly duckling will not have to find it for himself. It will be in the eyes and actions of everyone he meets.

Remember, love is God and God is loving, conscious, creative energy, or we would not be here discussing love and what we know about it.

Amen.

BERNIE SIEGEL, M.D.

As I sat down and began to write the Introduction for this book, I found myself going back to the thoughts of these contributors. I had asked them to write down the most important thing they knew about love, in the hope that we might all learn a little something from each other and because all my royalties would be pledged to helping children in need feel loved and happy and hopeful. Each new contribution that arrived brought me a thrill of surprise and yet a feeling of familiarity. These contributors have come from all walks of life—from preachers to politicians, from actors to artists. But each of their comments suggested that they find love in the simple fabric of life around them.

Distilling my own thoughts on love for this Introduction has been a challenge. I read carefully the words of our contributors, I listened thoughtfully to the reflections of friends and family, and I watched closely the acts of love that fill our world. What I have seen and heard and learned is that love is many things. To each of us at any moment, love can be something different—a feeling, an action, something we receive, something we give. It seems to be a collection of little things, easily given, that make all the difference in how we feel, how we behave toward one another, what our world is and will be. It is a "many splendored thing" that "makes the world go around."

Like the contributors to this book and people everywhere, I find many of love's lessons in the people right in front of me. I reflected on one day's beginning. I got my two-year-old daughter, Grace, out of bed. She greeted me with her usual big smile. Then my six-year-old, Sam, wandered bleary-eyed into the bedroom where my wife, Ann, was just waking up. Those two are slow risers, unlike my ten-year-old daughter, Ariane, and me. I bring Ann her morning coffee and *The New York Times*, which pleases her. Pretty soon, Sam, Ariane, and Ann are chuckling, and Grace is singing along with *Teletubbies*. I love those morning sounds. I stand in the doorway, and take a moment to watch them before I kiss my family goodbye. It is a wonderful way to start my day.

I wondered at that moment, What *is* the most important thing they know about love? In the days that followed, I asked my parents, my wife, and my children to share their thoughts with me. With their writings in hand, I concluded that we all need to share our thoughts on love with each other more often. Here's what my family had to say:

To Love ONE NEEDS TRUST
AND FORGIVNESS TO LAST FOR LIME

Allan Adrian

We endure because
love endures.
Lorraine Gillis Adrian

Love enables you to be all
that you can be and
to accomplish anything you
imagine.
                    Ann Hood

You have to
trust the person
    you love.
Ariane Adrain
Age 10

THE MOSt
IMPORTAIM
THINAING
I SLOVING
YOUR FAMILY
samadcain

My life has been shaped and blessed by many people: my parents, who first showed me how to love; my brothers and sisters; my wife and children and friends, all helping me to learn more. Rev. Rebecca Spencer read from the Bible in a recent sermon that each of us is "the salt of the earth, the light of the world." Just as the pinch of salt enriches and a small candle brightens the darkened room, she suggested, our choice to love enables the beloved and then shows the way. The countless acts of love by one human being for another that I see and hear and read about every day—each "light the way" for me and help me to then light the way for others.

My fondest hope is that the thoughts here will encourage us, inspire us, and challenge us to love, because I believe that love is an act that creates a ripple farther than the eye can see and a spirit that lives far beyond the beating heart.

THE MOST IMPORTANT THING

I KNOW ™

About Love

Love is like hash. You have to have confidence in it to enjoy it.

In 1933, Bob Hope was playing the male lead of Huckleberry Haines in *Roberta*. The show received mediocre reviews, but reviewers said Hope, still relatively unknown at that point, saved the show with his hilarious ad libs—remarks of which Jerome Kern, who wrote the play, was not too fond. In response to the female lead's now famous line and song, "In England, we have a saying: when you're in love, 'Smoke Gets in Your Eyes,'" Bob responded, "In America we say, 'Love is like hash. You have to have confidence in it to enjoy it.'" Over the past sixty years, Bob Hope has proven himself to be one of the greatest comedic entertainers, as well as one of the greatest humanitarians of all time. He set the world record for the longest-running contract with a single network when he retired from NBC in 1997, after sixty years of television and radio stardom. The product of a modest beginning, he was born in England in 1903. He immigrated to Cleveland with his family, and became a citizen in 1920. Shortly after, he began taking dancing lessons and a star was born. Hope is perhaps best known for his Christmas shows, and for all of his performances for American servicemen and women abroad. Currently, he remains happily married to his wife, Dolores Reade, and devoted to his four children and his grandchildren. He is living proof that life begins at ninety.

BOB HOPE

"Love is like hash. You have to have confidence in it to enjoy it."

-[adlib] Bob Hope as Huckleberry Haines in Jerome Kern's "Roberta" on Broadway 1933

Love brings us closer to perfection. It is the sun that lights up our life and warms that of others.

I love you!

Brigitte Bardot took the world by storm at the age of fifteen, when she appeared on the cover of *Elle* magazine. In the 1950s, she began a film career that climaxed in 1956 with *And God Created Woman*. During this time she was married to Roger Vadim, the film's director, who pushed Bardot's film persona as a sex kitten, an image still widely associated with her today. With her model appearance and her much-portrayed love life off-camera, some prominent feminists have praised her as a woman before her time, unafraid of basking in her sexuality. She retired from films in 1973, and since then she has been an activist for animal rights worldwide.

L'amour nous rapproche
de la perfection.
C'est le soleil qui illumine
notre vie et réchauffe celle
des autres.

je t'aime!

Brigitte Bardot

The Bible speaks of love for all as the "more excellent way." We must excel in compassion and reconciliation if we are to make a dangerous and divided world into a place where all can develop their God given gifts.

Rev. Dr. Joan Brown Campbell has distinguished herself as a spiritual leader with a dynamic ability to deliver moral messages. She has been the General Secretary of the National Council of Churches of Christ in the USA since 1991, the first female minister to serve in that position. She is an ordained minister in the Christian Church and the American Baptist Church, and Campbell has been a leading force in creating opportunities for cooperation with other churches, faiths, and related organizations. Campbell has taken leading roles in the Council for the past two decades, and she is in demand as a speaker and preacher on such topics as racism, women's rights, poverty, and Christian unity. She received her graduate degree from the Case Western Reserve School of Social Work, has studied at Bossey Ecumenical Institute in Geneva, Switzerland, and has been recognized with eight honorary degrees.

National Council of the Churches of Christ in the USA

Office of the
General Secretary

The Bible speaks of love for all as the
"more excellent way". We must excel in
compassion and reconciliation if we are
to make a dangerous and divided world
into a place where all can develop their
God given gifts.

Rev. D. Joan Brown Campbell
General Secretary
National Council of Churches of
Christ in USA.

Love cures, heals and rewards two people: the lover and the beloved.

Dr. Bernie S. Siegel was educated in traditional medicine at Colgate University and Cornell University Medical College. In June 1978, Siegel went through a life-changing experience when he met a group of doctors who used imagery techniques to fight cancer. When he tried meditation for the first time, Siegel admits, he was extremely skeptical; however, he found that a new world opened up to him. Since then he has become a leader in bringing awareness to healing, especially among cancer patients. He recommends such practices as Kundalini yoga, meditation, and healing circles. Dr. Siegel is the author of *Love, Medicine & Miracles* and *Peace, Love & Healing* and founder of EcaP (Exceptional Cancer Patients).

Bernard S. Siegel, MD.

Love cures, heals &
rewards two people:
the lover + the beloved.

Love

Bernie
Siegel

We love because it's the only true adventure.

I n an introduction to one of her many books of poetry, Nikki Giovanni's poems are referred to as "souvenirs collected from so many precious moments." She considers their value to be in the images and memories that they conjured. Through her poetry, Giovanni has documented four decades of her experience as a black woman. In the 1960s, her voice was rebellious, and her works splintered into images of passion and change. In the 1970s, she exchanged idealism for realism as her poetry emerged into a more mature womanhood, and since this time she has broken new ground repeatedly, as a black female poet and as an original voice. Since her graduation from Fisk University in Nashville, Tennessee, in 1967, Giovanni has received countless honorary degrees and held professorships at many universities. She has shared her written and spoken words in publications and concerts throughout the world. In 1989, she accepted a permanent position as Professor of English at Virginia Polytechnic Institute and State University.

Nikki Giovanni

We love because it's the only true
adventure
Nikki Giovanni

From birth to death our first responsibility on earth is to our family . . . immediate and extended. They are our joy, love, friends, strength and *our responsibility.*

A country is only as strong as its families.

At age sixteen, Barbara Pierce fell in love with the future president of the United States, George Bush. Mrs. Bush has often made the joke that she married well; through her marriage she has been able to promote a myriad of humanitarian efforts and charitable causes, lovingly and with great success. After losing a daughter to leukemia in 1953, she became an advocate for children with leukemia. Mrs. Bush is best known, however, for her devotion to family literacy projects. She believes that if more people were able to read and to express themselves through writing, many of our social problems would begin to resolve themselves. In 1990, she helped to develop the Barbara Bush Foundation for Family Literacy, and since then she has served as its Honorary Chair. She also spends much time encouraging people to read through her public appearances and fundraisers. Mrs. Bush remains devoted to her husband and her five children, two of whom have entered politics themselves.

Barbara Bush

From birth to death our first
responsibility on earth is to our
family ... immediate and extended.
They are our joy, love, friends,
strength and _our responsibility_.
a country is only as strong as its'
families.

Barbara Bush

I have been given the greatest gift by two wonderful parents: unconditional love.

George W. Bush became the first Texas governor to be elected to consecutive four-year terms on November 3, 1998, with a victory in which he won 250 of the 254 counties in Texas. He has dedicated himself to walking the road of the compassionate conservative, shaping his policies based on the principles of limited government, personal responsibility, strong families, and local control. He has prioritized education, and is making strong efforts to have every child read by third grade. Bush, the son and namesake of a president, was raised in Midland and Houston, Texas. He has an undergraduate degree from Yale University and an M.B.A. from Harvard Business School. After serving as an F-102 pilot for the Texas Air National Guard, he began a career in the oil and gas business in 1975. After completing work on his father's 1988 presidential campaign, he served as managing general partner of the Texas Rangers baseball team until he was elected governor in 1994. Bush lives with his wife, Laura, and his twin teenage daughters in Austin, Texas.

THE STATE OF TEXAS
GOVERNOR

*I have been
given the greatest
gift by two
wonderful parents:
Unconditional
Love -*

GEORGE W. BUSH

Unconditional love is the greatest gift you can give to yourself or to another.

In 1941, seven years before her marriage to future president Gerald R. Ford, Betty Ford transformed her love of dance into a dance group for handicapped children. After marrying the President, Mrs. Ford remained committed to the arts and children with disabilities. Having fought a brief bout with breast cancer in 1974, she became an advocate for women's issues, significantly raising breast cancer awareness. She is perhaps best known for the Betty Ford Center at Eisenhower Medical Center, which she opened in 1982, as a result of her own successful battle with chemical dependency. The Betty Ford Center remains at the forefront of treatment facilities in our nation, and Betty Ford continues to play an active, hands-on role as the chairman of the Board of Directors. Throughout her life, Betty Ford has used her experiences and positions to reach out to those around her in love and support.

BETTY FORD

" Unconditional love is
the greatest gift you can
give to yourself or to
another " Betty Ford

The most important thing I know is: to do more listening than talking.

The most important thing I know about love is: you get what you give.

Minnesota's First Lady, Terry Ventura, will be celebrating her twenty-fifth wedding anniversary to Governor Jesse Ventura this year. When Mrs. Ventura was only four, her family left their farm for city life in Minneapolis. At heart, however, she was still a country girl, and she returned to her grandparents' home every weekend to ride horses and help with chores. Mrs. Ventura met Jesse Ventura the year after she finished high school in 1974; ten months later, they were married. Today, they live on a ranch with their two teenage children, Tyrel and Jade, and all their other family members, including nine horses, eight chickens, three cats, and a bulldog. Recently, Terry Ventura has begun a breeding program for champion horses, and she and Jade enjoy showing their American Saddlebreds at horse shows across the state. As First Lady, Mrs. Ventura supports many humanitarian works, and is an advocate for the small family farm as well as special education programs.

Terry Ventura
First Lady

The most important thing
I know is: to do more
listening than talking.

The most important thing
I know about love is:
you get what you give.

Terry Ventura

Love, very simply, matters most.

N ora Roberts wrote her first romance novel in a spiral note-book with a number two pencil, having never been to col-lege. The book was born of boredom when she was confined to her house for a week, due to a nasty blizzard. Nearly twenty years later, she has written and published more than 130 novels. At 48, she is a romance superstar. In 1998, she had eleven titles on the *New York Times* hardcover and paperback bestseller lists, includ-ing four titles that hit number one. She was the first inductee into the Romance Writers of America Hall of Fame, and she has won awards too numerous to list. Nora feels that her heroines are strong, independent women, and wants her readers to see them-selves reflected in her writing.

Nora Roberts

Love, very simply, matters most.

Nora Roberts

The more people you fit *in* to your circle of love the more love there is for everybody in the circle . . . you don't even have to ration . . . there is always enough love to go around.

elen Gurley Brown has been a motivated writer from the start. At age fourteen, she wrote a letter to President Roosevelt about her sister, Mary, who suffered from polio. The letter was so persuasive and moving that the President started a communication with Mary, greatly lifting her spirits. Brown studied at Texas State College before moving to New York and entering advertising. She began as a secretary, and it was not until she won a contest through *Glamour* magazine that she was invited to write copy. During this time, she married David Brown and wrote her bestselling book, *Sex and the Single Girl*, a novel promoting the belief that young working women were independent and capable of all things. In response, Brown received mail from all over the country, and she spent night after night answering letters. One evening, David suggested that she create a magazine in which she could answer all of the letters openly. This idea was realized when Brown was invited to revive the magazine *Cosmopolitan*, at the age of forty-one. For the next thirty years, she served as editor-in-chief, creating the ultimate image of the "Cosmo Girl," a successful, independent woman. In addition, she has published several other books, including *Sex and the Office*, *Outrageous Opinions*, and *Having It All*.

HELEN GURLEY BROWN

The more people you fit in to
your circle of love the more love there
is for every Body in the circle ...
you don't even have to ration ...
there is always enough love
to go around

Helen Gurley Brown

Love is the most wonderful emotion anyone can have. To be genuine it must come from the heart. Then it permeates the entire body.

Love brings many rewards. It helps to create a feeling of self-worth. It motivates a giving spirit. It enhances a peaceful life. It helps to make living a great experience.

Ruth Stafford Peale has distinguished herself as a religious leader, author, and inspiring speaker. Her training began young, as she was the daughter of a prominent minister. Mrs. Peale received a degree from Syracuse University in 1930, and taught math until she married the late Dr. Norman Vincent Peale. She has inspired many Americans as the co-founder and chairman of the board of *Guideposts*. In addition, she serves on the boards of many influential organizations, and she holds the distinction of being the first woman president of the National Board of North American Missions of the Reformed Church in America. Mrs. Peale has written for many nationally syndicated magazines, and she is the author of *Secrets of Staying in Love*, published by Thomas Nelson.

Love is the most wonderful emotion anyone can have. To be genuine it must come from the heart. Then it permeates the entire body.

Love brings many rewards. It helps to create a feeling of self-worth. It motivates a giving spirit. It enhances a peaceful life. It helps to make living a great experience.

Ruth Stafford Peale

The Greek poet Sappho described love as bittersweet. It creates and destroys. Its mystery is as deep as its power is strong. Still, it is worth every risk.

For twelve years, Thomas Moore explored his spirituality as a monk with a Catholic religious order. Today, he has written two bestselling books, *Care of the Soul* and *Soul Mates*, that urge the American public to search for sacredness in everyday living. He sets out three principles for spiritual living: first, we have to find a way not to do so much; second, one must consider the importance of images, of being surrounded with vibrancy and color; and lastly, he suggests that one develop a spiritual practice. His writing explores these principles in practical terms, asserting that in order to move into the future we need to go backwards, abandoning the technological achievements of this century. Moore received his Ph.D. in Religious Studies from Syracuse University. In addition, he has completed studies in theology, musicology, and philosophy. He has also published several other articles and books, and he is currently a practicing psychotherapist.

THOMAS MOORE

The Greek poet Sappho described love as bittersweet. It creates and destroys. Its mystery is as deep as its power is strong. Still, it is worth every risk.

Thomas Moore

Being married to the Love of my Life, and watching him fall in love with our two baby girls day in and day out is such an example of total unconditional love and adoration. I am truly blessed.

Kris Jenner and her husband, Bruce, have become synonymous with health and fitness today. Born in San Diego, California, Kris was an avid athlete even as a child. Currently, she works alongside Bruce in their company, 8634 Inc., as vice president and chief operating officer. In addition, she is president of Jenner Communications. The Jenners are known for their popular infomercial series promoting a wealth of fitness-related products. Kris has made a number of television appearances, and she has been featured on the cover of *American Fitness Magazine* and *Beverly Hills Life*. The Jenners are devoted to family life with their six children, balancing the responsibilities of their demanding work with driving carpools, coaching soccer, and leading Brownies.

Kris and Bruce Jenner

Being married to the Love of my
Life, and watching him fall in love
with our two baby girls day in and
day out is such an example of
total unconditional love and
adoration. I am truly blessed.

Kris Jenner

Einstein once said: "No number of experiments can ever prove that I am right, but a single experiment, at any time, can prove that I am wrong."

If everybody felt the same way, i.e., that like in science, no truth is absolute and that they might be wrong, it would be the end of all political, ethnic, moral or religious fanaticism.

As a schoolchild in Geneva, Edmond H. Fischer, winner of the 1992 Nobel Prize in Physiology or Medicine, formed a lifelong friendship with Wilfried Haudenschild, an inventive, tinkering boy. Together they decided that one should take up medicine and the other should become a scientist. Dr. Fischer became the scientist, and his achievements have made history. After studying music at the Geneva Conservatory of Music, he went on to study chemistry just as World War II started. In the early 1950s, Dr. Fischer came to the United States, where he accepted a professorship at the University of Washington. It was here that he met Edwin G. Krebs, and the duo teamed up to examine uncharted territories. They are best known for their studies of the regulation of glycogen metabolism, which contributed to an understanding of the central role of phosphorylation mechanisms in the control of cellular events. Currently, he is still at the University of Washington, where he serves as a Professor Emeritus.

UNIVERSITY OF WASHINGTON

Edmond H. Fischer
Department of Biochemistry

Einstein once said: " No number of experiments can ever prove that I am right, but a single experiment, at any time, can prove that I am wrong."

If everybody felt the same way, i.e., that like in science, no truth is absolute and that they might be wrong, it would be the end of all political, ethnic, moral or religious fanaticism.

Edmond H. Fischer

I prefer to explore the most intimate moments, the smaller, crystallized details we all hinge our lives on.

Rita Dove's love affair with poetry began at age eleven when she found a gold and purple anthology of poetry at her local library. As she browsed through it, this book served as her connection to a world that belonged entirely to her. She was born in Akron, Ohio, to adoring parents who valued education strongly. From a young age, she loved poetry and music and playing the cello. After graduating as a Presidential Scholar, Rita Dove excelled at Miami University in Ohio, graduating summa cum laude in 1973 with a degree in English. She won a two-year Fulbright Scholarship to go to Germany before joining the famous Writer's Workshop at the University of Iowa. There she met her future husband, Fred Viebahn; their daughter, Aviva, was born in 1983. Rita Dove has gone on to win a Pulitzer Prize for her 1987 collection, *Thomas and Beulah*, and was named poet laureate of the United States in 1993. With her large number of publications, public appearances, and awards, Dove has proven herself to be one of the most influential African-American poets of our time. Currently, she is Commonwealth Professor of English at the University of Virginia in Charlottesville, Virginia.

RITA DOVE
Commonwealth Professor of English

Sylvie Moore,
Executive Secretary

Dept. of English

University of Virginia
Charlottesville, VA 22903

I prefer to explore The most intimate moments, the smaller, crystallized details we all hinge our lives on.

Rita Dove

Love is the energy of God. Pray for it, lavish it on others, receive it gratefully when it comes to you. Cultivate friendship like a garden. It is the best love of all.

Sister Helen Prejean grew up in a loving family in Baton Rouge, Louisiana, where she chose to join the Sisters of St. Joseph of Medaille. Prejean found that drawing into herself in prayer helped her to reach out to others, and her life has been dedicated to service. While living in the St. Thomas Housing Project in New Orleans, Sister Prejean naively agreed to be a pen pal to a man on Death Row, an agreement that would change her life forever. In April 1984, Sister Helen Prejean witnessed the death by electrocution of Patrick Sonnier, to whom she served as spiritual advisor. She would later refer to this event as a second baptism. As a result of the event, she wrote a book entitled *Dead Man Walking: An Eyewitness Account of the Death Penalty in the United States*, which spent thirty-one weeks on the *New York Times* bestseller list and was nominated for a Pulitzer Prize. Since this time, she has served as a strong advocate for ending the death penalty. Susan Sarandon starred in the film that documented her story, *Dead Man Walking*.

To: Corme A. Adrain
    The Most Important Thing I Know
From: Sister Helen Prejean

"
Love is the energy of God.
Pray for it, lavish it on others,
receive it gratefully when it
comes to you. Cultivate
friendship like a garden.
It is the best love of all. "

            Sister Helen Prejean, csj

I've been very blessed to be able to reach out to people's hearts with the music I write. I find it very powerful that the music I send out with love comes back to me with love.

Throughout the past fifty years, Burt Bacharach has written the definition of popular music, literally. He has written numerous hit songs, such as "Raindrops Keep Fallin' on My Head," "I'll Never Fall in Love Again," and "What the World Needs Now Is Love," as well as several notable films and musicals, including *What's New Pussycat?; Promises, Promises*; and *Arthur*. Bacharach was raised in New York, where he played in various jazz ensembles starting in the 1940s. After serving in the United States Army, Bacharach devoted himself to a career in piano arranging and songwriting. In the late 1950s, he teamed up with Hal David to form a partnership that wrote extraordinarily successful lyrics for great artists such as Marty Robbins, Perry Como, Frankie Vaughan, and perhaps most prominently, Dionne Warwick. Bacharach expanded his repertoire even more with his hit Broadway musical *Promises, Promises*. Bacharach, with his wife and partner for twelve years, Carole Bayer Sager, produced hit songs for Elton John, Stevie Wonder, and others.

BURT BACHARACH

I've been very blessed to be able to reach out to peoples hearts with the music I write. I find it very powerful that the music I send out with love comes back to me with love.

Burt Bacharach

"What the World Needs Now Is Love" is more than a title of one of my songs, it's what I believe each of us would and should share with one another.

When Dionne Warwick was recording Hal David's brilliant song of the mid-1960s, "What the World Needs Now," she made the comment that it should be the new national anthem. Over the past three decades, David's music has seeped into the nation's soul; along with his longtime partner, Burt Bacharach, he has been responsible for many of the popular music standards performed by such artists as Warwick, Willie Nelson, and Bette Midler. David has received nearly every award given by the music industry, including three Oscar nominations. Most recently, he won the Grammy Trustee Award of the National Academy of Recording Arts and Sciences. He has written numerous film scores, including *What's New Pussycat?*, *Alfie*, and *The Look Of Love*, and his and Bacharach's Broadway debut, *Promises, Promises*, received both a Grammy and a Tony nomination. In addition to his successful music career, David supports many charitable causes; he is the founder of the Los Angeles Music Center.

CASA DAVID

What the world needs now
is love is more than a
title of one of my songs, it is
what I believe each of us
wanted to share
with one another

Hal David

The sweetness of lasting intimacy grows out of the rockier terrain of self-discovery . . . Before you can be intimate with another, you must first dare to be intimate with yourself.

Sandra R. Scantling is helping people everywhere to achieve a greater sense of intimacy with their partners in her bestselling book, *Ordinary Women, Extraordinary Sex*. Dr. Scantling is a licensed clinical psychologist, as well as a certified sex therapist. In addition to her private practice in Connecticut, she is on the faculty of the University of Connecticut School of Medicine. Her videotape series, *Ordinary Couples, Extraordinary Sex*, is helping couples to reap the benefits of deeper emotional intimacy. Dr. Scantling has appeared on *Today* and *Good Morning America* to discuss her theories. She also has been quoted in popular magazines such as *Cosmopolitan*, *New Woman*, *Glamour*, and *Redbook*.

Sandra R. Scantling

The sweetness of lasting Intimacy grows out of the rockier terrain of self discovery --- Before you can be intimate with another, You must first dare to be intimate with Yourself.

Sandra Scantling

Love comes not from the material world but from the realm of the unseen. Its nurturing, therefore, requires not gifts which can be measured or weighed or bought or sold but only by gifts of the spirit.

As an inspirational Jewish leader, Rabbi Alexander M. Schindler has demonstrated uncompromising commitment to promoting social justice, peace, and equality in Judaism. He is the past president of the Union of American Hebrew Congregations, and he currently serves as the president of the Memorial Foundation for Jewish Culture and vice president of the World Jewish Congress. Rabbi Schindler understands Judaism to be a dynamic religion that evolves alongside tradition. Therefore, he has been an outspoken advocate for the equality of women in religious life, including rabbinical ordination. Also, he is nontraditional in welcoming non-Jewish spouses of Jews into the Jewish community and inviting them to embrace Judaism as a spiritual path. Rabbi Schindler has published *The Torah: A Modern Commentary*. He lives with his wife, Rhea Rosenblum, and their five children in Westport, Connecticut.

Rabbi Alexander M. Schindler

Love comes not from
the material world but
from the realm of the hidden.
Its nurturing, therefore, requires
not gifts which can be measured
or weighed or bought & sold
but only by gifts of the spirit.

Alexander Schindler

Love motivates.
Love inspires!
Love ignites!!
Love is awesome!!!

By age twenty-nine, Millard Fuller was a self-made millionaire with a failing marriage, suffering health, and compromised integrity. Fuller was born in Alabama, where he had worked his way through Auburn University, as well as Alabama Law School. Faced with a challenge to redefine success for himself, he reconciled his marriage, and he and his wife renewed their commitment to God. The Fullers found that the best way to exercise their understanding of the New Testament was to minister through action; as a result, the most successful service project in the history of the nation, Habitat for Humanity, was born. After working in small grass-roots initiatives in the U.S. and in Zaire (currently the Democratic Republic of Congo), Fuller led the initiative to form Habitat for Humanity in 1976. Over the past quarter of a century, 350,000 people have moved into homes built throughout the United States, as well as sixty countries worldwide, and Habitat is one of the largest builders in the U.S.

Millard Fuller

Love motivates,
Love inspires!
Love ignites!!
Love is awesome !!!

Millard Fuller

Love is my *decision* to make your problem my concern.

In 1955, with only $500 in assets and his wife, Arvella, to serve as organist, Robert Schuller rented the Orange Drive-in Theater in Garden Grove, California, in order to form the world's first walk-in-drive-in church. Schuller was ordained by the Reformed Church in America in 1950, and since then, millions of people have found encouragement and inspiration through his ministry. His church service, televised each week as the *Hour of Power,* is the most broadly televised church service in the world. Garden Grove, California, still hosts his original congregation, now boasting over ten thousand members and worshipping in the famous Crystal Cathedral, composed entirely of glass. Dr. Schuller has written thirty-two books, and businesses and conferences worldwide seek him for his motivational speaking.

ROBERT SCHULLER

Love is my
decision to
make your
problem my
concern. Robert Schuller

I always finish all my books with: "They found Love, Real Love, which comes from God, is part of God, and was theirs for Eternity."

I n 1940, at the height of World War II, Barbara Cartland sailed to the safety of Canada with her three children to stay with friends. She insisted on returning to England, complaining that it was not fair that she should be protected when so many were not. Despite much protest by her government, she succeeded in her demands and returned to England. This strength of purpose is a defining characteristic of her personality; Cartland is a dynamic, invigorating woman who has proven herself to be one of the most prolific writers of all time, as well as a champion for charitable causes. For decades, Cartland set the world record every year for publishing the most novels, with an average of twenty-three per year. She has currently written more than six hundred books, among them *We Danced All Night* and *The Magic of Honey*. She has received the Gold Medal of Paris, the highest award given by the prime minister, and in 1991 was invested by Her Majesty the Queen as Dame of the Order of the British Empire for her humanitarian work and her great contributions to literature.

From: Dame Barbara Cartland, D.B.E. D.St.J.

Dear Mr Adrain,

Thank you very much for your letter.

I think your book 'The Most Important Thing I know about Love' is a wonderful idea.

I always finish all my books with:

'They found Love, Real Love, which comes from God, is part of God, and was theirs for Eternity.'

With all my best wishes for a successful publication.

Tell 'em you love 'em while you can!

One of the most successful country singers of all time and a shrewd businesswoman, Loretta Lynn had a humble beginning. She was born in a wooden shack in Butcher Hollow, Kentucky, where she married at age thirteen, was a mother of three by seventeen, and had a grandchild by thirty-one. Her husband first encouraged her music career with the gift of a cheap guitar and gigs at local music halls. In 1960, she signed her first single, "I'm a Honky-Tonk Girl," with a small label, the beginning of a wealth of hits that would capture the hearts of country-western fans across the world for the next thirty years. As documented in her bestselling song, autobiography, and Oscar-winning movie, *Coal Miner's Daughter,* Loretta Lynn has made it through tough times without letting discouragement bring her down.

Loretta Lynn

"Tell 'em you love 'em while you can!"

Loretta Lynn

Imagine!

Born in Tokyo in 1933, Yoko Ono spent her childhood years traveling between Japan and the United States. She went to Sarah Lawrence College in 1953 to study music theory, but later switched to the Juilliard School, where she met her first husband, Toshi Ichiyanagi. In 1961, their marriage ended, and shortly after, she met her second husband, Anthony Cox. Kyoko, her first child, was born in 1963. While in London in 1966, she met the man she referred to as the love of her life, John Lennon. Their close friendship evolved into love by 1968, and on March 20, 1969, the world witnessed their wedding. The couple collaborated together musically and politically with such projects as their hit single, "Give Peace a Chance," which topped the charts. Their relationship grew turbulent in the early 1970s, but by 1975 they were strongly together, and they retired from music to raise their new son, Sean, full-time. In 1980, the duo publicly reemerged with the album *Double Fantasy*. Shortly after, however, Lennon was assassinated, and Ono's life changed dramatically. After disappearing for a couple of years, she returned to her career in experimental art and music.

Imagine!

Sve.
Yoko Ono '99

Love should be given unselfishly and without expectations, otherwise you continually will be disappointed.

In 1980, Candace Lightner lost her thirteen-year-old daughter Cari to a tragedy that should not have happened. Cari and a friend were walking along a city street when Cari was hit and killed by a man who had been out of jail for only two days. In his past were three Driving While Intoxicated arrests and two convictions. His sentence for Cari's death was lenient, and he was quickly on the streets again. Candace Lightner transformed her anger and loss into a national organization to inform, educate, and prevent such tragedies, Mothers Against Drunk Driving. In the eight years she headed the organization, it grew from a group of enraged activists to a large-scale nonprofit volunteer organization. By 1990, it had over four hundred chapters across the United States, and currently there are three million supporters. Lightner has promoted preventive measures for similar accidents and provided support through lectures, speeches, writings, and personal appearances. She has made television appearances, spoken before Congress, and worked as a consultant. She has published *Guilty Until Proven Innocent* and *Who's Responsible?* and is the recipient of the President's Volunteer Action Award.

From the desk of
Candace Lightner

Love should be given unselfishly
and without expectations, otherwise
you continually will be disappointed

Candace Lightner
Founder / MADD

My own personal core contains the music I've learned and loved. I use a centering exercise that reiterates the circular journey to the evolving self, and to loving, to communication, connection and healing.

Marni Nixon began her first music lessons on the violin at age four. By fourteen, she was appearing in plays at the famed Pasadena Playhouse, and she made her debut vocal soloist performance with the Los Angeles Philharmonic in Mozart's *Requiem* at age seventeen. Perhaps Nixon is most popularly known as the performer who dubbed the singing voices of such movie stars as Deborah Kerr in *The King and I* and *An Affair to Remember*, Audrey Hepburn *in My Fair Lady*, and Natalie Wood in *West Side Story*. However, these roles comprise only a minor element of her career. Nixon has appeared in musical comedy, cabaret, and motion pictures, and is an opera singer, stage actress, and recording artist. She has sung recitals, performed with symphonies, and made television appearances. During her versatile career as a singer and actress, she has been awarded two Gold Records, two classical Grammy Award nominations, and four Emmy Awards. Ms. Nixon has three children and five grandchildren, and she resides in New York City, where she continues to perform and teach privately and give master classes.

Marni Nixon

My own personal core contains
the music I've learned and loved.
I use a centering exercise that
reiterates the circular journey
to the evolving self, and to
loving, to communication,
connection and healing.

Cheers!

Marni Nixon

The most important things I've learned about love are that everyone and everything in this universe needs it, and that loving is even more important than being loved.

At age thirteen, Andrew Gold wrote his first songs and began to study a variety of musical instruments such as guitar, keyboards, and drums. His talent had a history: his father, Ernest Gold, was an Academy Award–winning composer (*Exodus*), and his mother, Marni Nixon, was the singing voice behind Natalie Wood in *West Side Story* and Audrey Hepburn in *My Fair Lady*. In 1973, Andrew joined Linda Ronstadt's band and spent much of the decade playing, singing, and arranging for her and others. He is particularly known for Ronstadt's "You're No Good" and "When Will I Be Loved," and Art Garfunkel's "I Only Have Eyes for You." The 1970s also saw four solo albums from him. They yielded two hit singles, "Lonely Boy" and "Thank You for Being a Friend," which eventually became TV's *Golden Girls* theme song. In the 1980s, his band with Graham Gouldman (of 10cc fame) was named WAX, and had an international hit with "Bridge to Your Heart." He has produced, written for, played, and sung on many movie soundtracks and television themes. He sings the theme song for *Mad About You*, and occasionally does the voice for Alvin of *Alvin and the Chipmunks* fame. He continues to tour, write, record, produce, and write hit songs for others, such as Wynnona Judd's "I Saw the Light," and Celine Dion's "Show Some Emotion." Andrew lives in Connecticut with his wife and three daughters.

ANDREW GOLD

THE MOST IMPORTANT
THINGS I'VE LEARNED ABOUT LOVE
ARE THAT EVERYONE AND EVERYTHING
IN THIS UNIVERSE NEEDS IT AND THAT
LOVING IS EVEN MORE IMPORTANT
THAN BEING LOVED

When you forget the truth of what love is, you will live the reality of what it is not.

Iyanla Vanzant, lawyer, bestselling author, and hailed as one of the "most dynamic African-American speakers in the country" by *Emerge* magazine, is a nationally recognized inspirational speaker, devoted to showing others the way to transform their lives. A teenage mother on welfare, an abused and battered wife, Iyanla has defied odds, becoming the author of books like *Yesterday, I Cried* and *One Day My Soul Just Opened Up*. Vanzant's personal experiences have given her profound insight into life. After she left her abusive husband, Vanzant went to Medgar Evers College and City University of New York Law School. She moved to Philadelphia with her children and practiced as a public defender for three years. She later became an ordained minister, committed to a message based on the principles of divine power and self-determination. She was also awarded an Oni by the International Congress of Black Women as one of the nation's unsung heroes and currently serves as a national spokesperson for Literacy Volunteers of America. The founder and executive director of Inner Visions Spiritual Life Maintenance Network, she conducts workshops and lectures to thousands around the country, hoping to inspire each listener to take a stand and create a better life, a better community, and a better world.

Iyanla

When you forget the truth
of what love is;
You will live the reality
of what it is not.

Iyanla

The real meaning of Christmas is the giving of love every day.

R ay Conniff's musical contributions have been striking a chord with the public for over fifty years. Conniff was born in 1916 to local musicians in Attleboro, Massachusetts. He began playing trombone and arranging music in high school, and worked his way through the Boston scene quickly. At the advice of a friend, he headed for New York just as swing was emerging. He played with some big names, like Bunny Berigan, Bob Crosby, Art Hodes, and Artie Shaw, before serving in the U.S. Army. After his discharge, Columbia Records hired him as an arranger; this was the start of a prolific and successful forty-year relationship. Conniff's debut album, *S'Wonderful*, was in the Top 20 for nine months. Throughout the 1960s, he enjoyed booming sales, and his concerts made national headlines for innovative use of live stereo. At eighty-two, Conniff has recorded one hundred albums, sold 65 million records, and received a Grammy. He has ten gold albums and numerous other awards, including CBS Records' International Crystal Globe Award. In March 1997, Conniff left Columbia Records to sign a contract with Polygram Records. Currently, he has released his third album on this label, *My Way*.

A doctor once told me
    L = Listen
    O = Observe
    V = Value
    E = Empathize

Reverend Monsignor Thomas J. Hartman, more popularly known as Father Tom, is the co-host, along with Rabbi Marc Gellman, of the popular television show *God Squad*. He also makes frequent appearances on *Good Morning America* and the *Imus in the Morning* radio show. In addition to numerous television and radio appearances, Hartman has authored several books, including *Just a Moment—Life Matters with Father Tom* and *The Matter of Life and Death*. The book *How Do You Spell God? Answers to the Big Questions from Around the World*, which he coauthored with Gellman, includes a foreword by the Dalai Lama. Father Tom's recognitions include three Emmy Awards, a Folio Award, and many Man of the Year Awards. He is the Director of Radio and Television for the Diocese of Rockville Centre. Father Tom holds an undergraduate degree in philosophy and a graduate degree in theology. In 1970, he received a master of divinity degree from Our Lady of Angels Seminary, and in 1979, he received a doctor of ministry degree from the Jesuit School of Theology at Berkeley.

REV. MSGR. THOMAS J. HARTMAN
DIRECTOR OF RADIO & TELEVISION

A doctor once told me

L = LISTEN

O = OBSERVE

V = VALUE

E = EMPATHIZE

Much love—

Fr. Tom Hartman

Love is magic—give it away and watch it return!

One of the world's most distinguished and prolific recording artists, Jessye Norman is known for her work in the operatic world. She has performed at all the major opera houses, including La Scala, the Metropolitan Opera, the Royal Opera House, Covent Garden, Stuttgart Opera, the Vienna and Hamburg State Operas, Opera Company of Philadelphia, and the Lyric Opera of Chicago, and appeared in the Aix-en-Provence Festival and the Salzburg Festival. Born in Augusta, Georgia, Ms. Norman started singing in church at the age of four. She was educated at Howard University in Washington, the Baltimore Conservatory, and the University of Michigan. After musical studies in America, she went to Europe, making her operatic debut in Berlin in 1969. She first appeared in America in 1972, in a concert performance of *Aida* at the Hollywood Bowl; her debut at the Metropolitan Opera came in *Les Troyens* in 1983. She has a commanding stage presence and she is widely acclaimed for the rich, "oceanic" tone she has brought to her repertoire, ranging from Mozart to Wagner to African-American spirituals.

JESSYE NORMAN

Love is magic —
give it away and
watch it settle!

Jessye Norman

The most important thing I know about love, is that it is often confused with sex. The more love there is around, the better everything is.

Phyllis Diller has done it all, literally. Her stage career did not begin until she was thirty-seven, after having given birth to five children. Millions of fans have supported her from around the world during her thirty-five years in show business. She has performed her spitfire comedy routines in nearly every major club in the United States. In addition, she has had roles in sixteen movies, including *Splendor in the Grass* and *Boy, Did I Get a Wrong Number!*, and numerous television shows, and has recorded five comedy albums. Diller has written four bestselling books, including *The Joys of Aging—And How to Avoid Them* and *Old Time Radio Comedy*. She has performed piano solos with one hundred symphony orchestras nationwide, and is currently developing her entrepreneurial skills with new ventures into chili (Phyllis Diller's Original Recipe), beauty products (La Vie), and jewelry (Phyllis Diller's Creations). On top of this, she has made a firm commitment to helping people throughout her life, and has been honored by countless organizations for her commitment to patriotic, philanthropic, and humanitarian efforts.

Phyllis Diller

The most important
thing I know about
love, is that it is
often confused with
sex. The more love
there is around, the
better everything is.

Phyllis Diller

It's the wind and the rain that come and scratch the face
It's the summery sun which softly burns the flesh
It's the calmed ocean waves that caress the beach
It's the child's quiet sleep in his baby carriage
It's the tired soldier who gets rid of his gun
It's the lost traveler who at last finds his way
It's the fruit just ripened and the wheat when it grows
It's the lighthouse that shines for the sailor at sea
It's the anxious poet finally finding his rhyme
It's the heaven and hell it's the devil and God
It's also deep inside us more intimate things
That help the heart to beat, and light flames in the eyes
Love is all that and much more personal things
That each one holds inside and hardly suspects,
Some that we've always known and others we ignore
That we can, if we want, find it deep in ourselves.

Born in Paris to Armenian parents, Charles Aznavour has been singing since age nine. He has toured in over eighty countries, six hundred of his songs have achieved Gold Record status, and he was the recipient of a Crystal Star Award. His efforts to aid Armenians after the 1988 catastrophic earthquake in Armenia led to his title of Ambassador-at-Large, granted in 1993. Most recent, Jacques Chirac, the French president, awarded Aznavour the title of Officier de la legion d'honneur, the highest distinction in all of France.

REPUBLIC OF ARMENIA

CHARLES AZNAVOUR
Ambassador at Large

C'est le vent et la pluie qui griffent le visage
C'est le soleil d'été qui vient brûler la peau
C'est l'océan calmé qui caresse la plage
C'est l'enfant endormi calme dans son landau
C'est le soldat lassé qui dépose son glaive
Le voyageur perdu qui trouve son chemin
C'est le fruit qui mûrit et c'est le blé qui lève
C'est le phare qui luit pour guider le marin
C'est le poète inquiet qui trouve enfin sa rime
C'est le ciel et l'enfer le diable et le bon Dieu
C'est aussi entre nous des choses plus intimes
Qui font battre les cœurs et font briller les yeux.
L'amour c'est tout cela et même plus encore
Que chacun porte en lui et ne soupçonne pas
De choses que l'on sait, d'autres que l'on ignore
Que l'on peut si l'on veut trouver au fond de soi.

76-78, avenue des Champs-Elysées, 75008 Paris

Love is helping people. God gives only time and wisdom in your life. Use it wisely to help others.

In 1948, the whole world tuned into the plight of one little boy's battle with cancer, as he sang "Take Me Out to the Ballgame" on national radio, and had the chance to speak to Ted Williams, his favorite member of the Boston Red Sox. Millions of listeners sent contributions to help Jimmy and children like him; their contributions became the basis of the Jimmy Fund, which supported Dr. Sidney Farber's work at Boston's Dana-Farber Cancer Institute. Dana-Farber has been instrumental in improving the cure rates for childhood cancer over the past fifty years, from less than 10 percent to over 70 percent. "Jimmy" was the name used to protect twelve-year-old Einar Gustafson of New Sweden, Maine, who was one of the first children to undergo chemotherapy. He is now a coast-to-coast truck driver, as well as a father and grandfather.

Love is helping
people. God gives only
time and wisdom in
your life.
   Use it wisely to
help others.
         Lina Gustafson
            "Jimmy"

Love is a fragile rose that withers without attention.

Lee Greenwood skipped his own high school graduation ceremony to perform at a showroom in Nevada. From the Sacramento farm where he grew up, Greenwood began perfecting his musical abilities, especially the saxophone. In high school, he formed his first band, the Moonbeams. For years he met with success in the Nevada lounge circuit as a musician by night and a blackjack dealer by day. In 1978, he formed a relationship with the head of MCA Publishing, and their first session together yielded the single "It Turns Me Inside Out," which stayed on the charts for twenty-two weeks. He was twice voted the Country Music Association's Male Vocalist of the Year. Greenwood's patriotic album, *God Bless the U.S.A.*, was used in both Bush and Reagan's presidential campaigns. In April 1996, after thirteen years of successful touring and twenty albums, Greenwood opened the Lee Greenwood Theater in Sevierville, Tennessee, to showcase his musical talents. There he has the opportunity to spend time with his wife, Kimberly, and their sons, Dalton and Parker.

LJ

love is a fragile
rose that withers
without attention.

[signature]

Never confuse passion with love. True love combines passion, forgiveness, understanding, and patience in equal parts.

When Christine Todd Whitman took office for her first term as New Jersey governor in 1993, she was the first woman to defeat an incumbent governor in a general election in modern state history. Judging from her reelection in 1997, as well as the policy changes she has made during her time in office, she has proven herself to be an effective and appreciated leader. Whitman has simultaneously cut income taxes and increased jobs. She has enacted tough anti-crime laws, buckled down on welfare reform, and implemented new educational standards, and she's responsible for more than half of preserved New Jersey land. Whitman was born in New York City in 1946, and raised in New Jersey. She received her bachelor's degree from Wheaton College in 1968, and served as both director of the Somerset County Board of Freeholders and president of the New Jersey Board of Public Utilities before becoming governor. Currently, she lives with her husband and their two children in Oldwick, New Jersey.

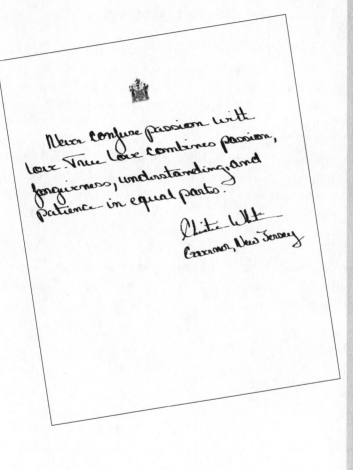

Never confuse passion with
love. True love combines passion,
forgiveness, understanding, and
patience — in equal parts.

Christie Whit
Governor, New Jersey

For me, love is compassion for mankind, respect of nature: the lack of either makes life an obscenity.

rnest J. Gaines has distinguished himself as an American writer, reflecting poignantly the African-American experience derived from his rural Louisiana childhood. He has constructed a fictional plantation area called Bayonne, which has been compared to Faulkner's imaginary Yoknapatawpha County. Born in Oscar, Louisiana, in 1933, he moved to California by the time he was fifteen. In 1957, he graduated from San Francisco State College, and went on to graduate school at Stanford University. Gaines taught and was a writer-in-residence at Dennison and Stanford, among others. Mr. Gaines's most acclaimed work, *The Autobiography of Miss Jane Pittman* (1971), reflects the African-American life history and the word-of-mouth customs of his Louisiana childhood. His other titles include *Catherine Carmier, Of Love and Dust, In My Father's House*, and *A Gathering of Old Men*.

Ernest J. Gaines

For me, love is Compassion
for mankind, respect of Nature:
the lack of either maker like
an Obscenity.

Ernest J. Gaines

The most important thing I know about love: Love is the essential ingredient in the cookie of life.

Mort Walker sold his first cartoon at age eleven. Born Addison Morton Walker in 1923, he grew up in El Dorado, Kansas. In high school, Walker used funds from cartoons he sold to finance his dating life. By the time he was eighteen, he was the chief editorial designer for Hall Brothers, designers of Hallmark cards. In 1942, having finished only a year and a half of college, Walker left to join the armed services. He was discharged in 1946, and completed his degree at the University of Missouri in 1948. His first big break came in 1950 when his comic strip *Beetle Bailey* was accepted for syndication. Though it was slow to start, the outbreak of the Korean War saw a jump in its popularity. At that time the Tokyo edition of the Army newspaper, *Stars and Stripes*, discontinued running Bailey because it had a poor conception of soldiers. In response, newspapers and magazines around the world picked up the strip, and the American public was in an uproar. In 1954, Walker launched a spinoff of Beetle, *Hi and Lois*. Walker has won countless awards, and he is the founder of the Museum of Cartoon Art in Rye Brook, New York.

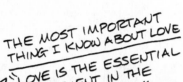

THE MOST IMPORTANT
THING I KNOW ABOUT LOVE

"LOVE IS THE ESSENTIAL
INGREDIENT IN THE
COOKIE OF LIFE."

MORT
WALKER

Love is the most powerful force known to mankind. More powerful even than its polar opposite—which is fear.

LeVar Burton, multitalented film star and director, did not intend to go into acting originally. At the age of thirteen, he entered Catholic seminary with ambitions to join the priesthood. Four years later, however, he left the seminary to accept a full academic scholarship at the University of Southern California, where he pursued a bachelor of fine arts degree. While only a sophomore, he landed his first role, as Kunta Kinte in the award-winning miniseries *Roots*. This earned him an Emmy nomination for Best Leading Actor. After acting in several TV films and miniseries, he began hosting the popular children's show *Reading Rainbow*, which is now in its seventeenth season. In addition to acting, he has a busy career as a producer/director, having directed episodes of the *Star Trek* series. Fans may recognize him from the series as Geordi LaForge. His production company, Eagle Nations Films, has signed a deal with Paramount Pictures to produce television and feature films. Also, in 1997, Burton debuted as an author with his novel, *Aftermath*, a science fiction thriller from Warner Books. In 1988, Burton married Stephanie Cozart, and their daughter, Michaela, is four.

LeVar Burton

Love is the most powerful force
known to mankind. More powerful
even than its polar opposite —
which is fear.

True love is unconditional; it is forgiving; it is God's greatest gift to man.

James A. Baker III has served in senior government posts for nearly two decades. He first joined the presidential staff as undersecretary of commerce to President Gerald Ford in 1975. From 1981 until 1985, he served as White House chief of staff to President Reagan. Under President George Bush, Baker served as the nation's sixty-first secretary of state. During his time in the State Department, he traveled to ninety foreign countries in an effort to negotiate the challenges presented in the aftermath of the cold war. His time concluded with his role as White House Chief of Staff and Senior Counselor to President Bush in 1992–93. Baker, a Houston native, graduated from Princeton University in 1952. He served in the U.S. Marine Corps for two years before entering The University of Texas School of Law at Austin, where he graduated with honors in 1957. Baker has received numerous distinctions, the most notable being the Presidential Medal of Freedom in 1991. He and his wife have returned to Houston, where they have eight children.

James A. Baker, III

True love is unconditional;
it is forgiving; it is God's
greatest gift to man.
                    Jim Baker

When it comes to love . . . never be reckless with someone else's heart. And, don't put up with someone else being reckless with yours!

Ruby Bridges's first day of first grade was one of the most memorable dates in the civil rights movement. In September 1960, she walked past hostile crowds of protestors, many of whom were shouting death threats. She became the first African-American student to attend William Frantz School in New Orleans, opening the doors to school integration. As a result, her dad was fired from his job, and her grandparents were forced to leave the farm where they had been sharecroppers for thirty years. Ruby Bridges-Hall gives the credit for her action to her parents, and all the sacrifices they made for her education. Ultimately, her actions would benefit all students in America. Now she spends her life reaching out to others to encourage them to play an active part in the education of their children.

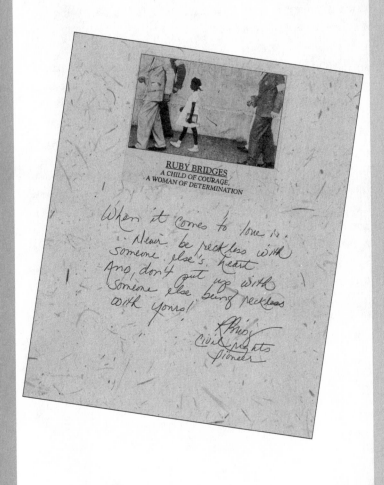

RUBY BRIDGES
A CHILD OF COURAGE,
A WOMAN OF DETERMINATION

When it comes to love is
... Never be reckless with
someone else's heart
And, don't put up with
someone else being reckless
with yours!

Ruby
Civil rights
pioneer

A lot of things matter, if we care. Love is the only thing that must matter, or we can't care.

During his college days at Princeton, Frank Deford's basketball coach took a moment to tell him that he wrote basketball better than he played it—so he left playing to begin writing. Several decades later, Deford is still writing basketball, as well as a number of other sports. He can be heard every Wednesday on National Public Radio's newsmagazine *Morning Edition*, where he has worked as a commentator since 1980, with one exception: in the early 1990s, he left NPR as well as his successful career with *Sports Illustrated* to publish the nation's first sports newspaper. He returned to NPR in 1991 because it gave him a different audience, a group of listeners who may not have tuned into the sports world without his commentary. Deford has been seen as a sports commentator on NBC and CNN, and he has written several movie and television scripts and two books. Deford lives in Westport, Connecticut, with his wife, Carol, and their two children.

FRANK DEFORD

A lot of things matter, if we care.
Love is the only thing that must matter,
or we can't care.

Frank Deford

My parents taught me, by example, the most important things about love—love is unconditional, patient, kind, generous, self-sacrificing and forever!

Elaine Chao is proof that American women make powerful, effective leaders. She is perhaps best known for her time as the president and CEO of United Way of America. Upon her arrival in 1992, UWA's future was threatened by mismanagement, but she used the following four years to raise funds and increase public confidence in UWA, turning it around entirely. Before that, in addition to several other positions in federal government, Chao served as director of the Peace Corps, venturing into uncharted territories with the commencement of programs in several Eastern European countries. Chao received an M.B.A. degree from the Harvard School of Business after completing her undergraduate work at Mount Holyoke College. Currently she is a distinguished fellow at the well-known policy research institute in Washington, The Heritage Foundation. She lives with her husband, Mitch McConnell, one of Kentucky's senators, and their three daughters.

Elaine L. Chao

My parents taught me, by example, the most important things about love ~ love is unconditional, patient, kind, generous, self-sacrificing and forever!

E.L. Chao

Love is at its best when it is given unconditionally—the way I love my wife, daughters, and family.

itch McConnell's leadership ability was recognized at a young age when he was elected president of his high school class. Born and raised in South Louisville, Kentucky, he is now one of the state's most popular senators. McConnell is the only Republican in Kentucky to have been elected to the Senate three times; his activism during his time in office can be seen through his involvement in several committees, including the National Republican Senatorial Committee (NRSC), of which he is the chairman. McConnell's outspoken views have made him a popular commentator both on television and in the press, and *George* magazine recently named him one of Washington's fifty most powerful people. He is married to Elaine L. Chao, and they have three daughters.

MITCH McCONNELL
KENTUCKY

United States Senate
WASHINGTON, D. C. 20510

Love is at its best when
it is given inconditionally -
the way I love my wife,
daughters, and family.

Mitch McConnell

If you are nice to everyone, they will be nice to you once they overcome their suspicion of why you are being nice.

In 1997, Ben Carson flew to South Africa to perform an operation in which he successfully separated a pair of Siamese twins who were joined at the head, a moment he has come to think of as one of his most crucial. In 1994, he had made a trip to the same place for the same reason, but the twins did not survive. With an unruly temper and poor grades, Carson began his academic career as the class "dummy." However, his mother was influential in providing him with a strong sense of self-discipline. He used this discipline to gain acceptance into Yale, and eventually into the University of Michigan Medical School, from which he graduated in 1977. After a residency at Johns Hopkins Hospital in Baltimore, Carson and his wife, Candy, lived in Australia for a year. Upon their return in 1983, Ben was appointed head of the hospital's pediatric neurosurgery department. Since that time, he has gained acclaim for his success in extraordinarily difficult procedures, becoming the nation's top pediatric neurosurgeon. Dr. Carson attributes much of his success to his strong faith. This faith spans his work life as well as his life with Candy and their three sons.

JOHNS HOPKINS
M E D I C I N E

Neurological Surgery

Benjamin S. Carson, Sr., M.D.
Director, Pediatric Neurosurgery

If you are nice to everyone,
they will be nice to you
once they overcome their
suspicion of why you
are being nice.

Ben Carson MD

Love is the best hope—the only hope—we have for the world. Its power continues to astonish me.

Susan Elizabeth Phillips has captured the hearts and minds of romance readers across America with her books that combine love and humor. Her books are being released and rereleased at the rate of about one per year. Phillips's first book was published in 1982. After that, she published four women's fiction books before settling into a series of romantic comedies, which began with *It Had to Be You*. Many of her recent works center around the adventures of a mythical football team, and a series of people connected to them. At a time when many romance authors are selling out to write books that are more mainstream and may sell better, Susan Elizabeth Phillips remains emphatically committed to writing about relationships. It is obvious through her work that she loves what she does.

Susan Elizabeth Phillips

Love is the best hope —
the only hope — we have
for the world. Its
power continues to
astonish me.

Susan Elizabeth Phillips

Love is both the call of the wild and the most civilizing force in humanity.

uis Rodriguez rescued himself from the tough gang life of East Los Angeles through poetry and prose. In 1993, he documented his story in the award-winning novel *Always Running, La Vida Loca: Gang Days in L.A.* Rodriguez published this novel to help his son, Ramiro, who struggled with gangs despite his father's activism, and for all of his friends on the street. Luis Rodriguez is the founder and a board member of Youth Struggling for Survival, and he has appeared in peacemaking roles at various historic gang summits. Also, Rodriguez's poetry is internationally recognized. He is a contributor to *Hungry Mind Review*, and the founder of Tia Chucha Press. His latest work, a children's illustrated and bilingual book, was released last year.

Luis J. Rodriguez

Love is both the call of the wild
And the most civilizing force
in humanity.

L. J. Rodriguez

Love is not said with your lips. Love is not said with your pen. Love is said with your heart.

Over forty years ago, Gwen Grant Mellon and her husband, William Larimer Mellon, left their life of comfort on a ranch in Arizona for the unknown land of Haiti. Inspired by Albert Schweitzer's philosophy of "Reverence for Life" and the hospital he had constructed in Africa, Mr. Mellon went to medical school in Louisiana, while Gwen traveled to Haiti with their four young children to build a hospital. With 110 beds and a staff that is 95 percent Haitian, the Mellons worked hard to create a hospital community that supports the health of the Haitian people. Dr. Mellon passed away in 1989, but Gwen Grant Mellon has continued to oversee hospital operations tirelessly, attending work each day, even as she approaches ninety years old. With a quiet dedication, she concentrates on hospital business, fulfilling the dream she shared with her husband to live with and serve the people of Haiti.

Mrs. William Larimer Mellon, Jr.
Deschapelles, Haiti

Love is not said with
your lips
Love is not said with
your pen
Love is said with your
heart

Gwen Grant Mellon

The most important thing I know about love is

1. There isn't enough in the world

2. It is the most important thing we can give each other

Carole Bayer Sager, a native of New York, is most proud of the work she did to raise money for AIDS research just as the crisis was reaching national recognition. She collaborated with songwriters and artists such as Elton John and Stevie Wonder to write and perform the song "That's What Friends Are For." This Academy Award–winning songwriter has produced some of the best-loved music of the past quarter century, including "Through the Eyes of Love" from the film *Ice Castles*. She's teamed with such songwriting marvels as Burt Bacharach and Linda Thompson Foster. She has written for films such as Clint Eastwood's *True Crimes* and *Quest for Camelot*. Currently, she is coproducing an album for Carole King and working with Michael Jackson on his latest album.

Carole Bayer Sager

The most important thing I know
about love is —
1. There isn't enough in
   the world —
2. it is the most important
   thing we can give eachother

Carole Bayer Sager

Without love, we are nothing—with love, we can accomplish miracles!

Dina Merrill, daughter of New York financier E. F. Hutton and cereal heiress Marjorie Merriweather Post, left acting on Broadway to marry in 1946, convinced that it was the more appropriate step for a young woman. A decade later, however, she had left the traditional life to return to acting. Merrill has dozens of film credits, including roles in *Butterfield 8* and *Operation Petticoat*. Since then, Merrill has acted in hundreds of television shows, and Broadway has made her a star. Her talents stretch past the screen, however, and into the business world; she is founding partner of Greenroom Enterprises and vice chairman of RKO Pictures (where she is the on-camera host for the PBS series *Decor*). Merrill is a strong supporter of the arts, and she supports many humanitarian efforts. Together with her husband, Ted Hartley, Merrill founded the Story Project, an organization that aspires to improve teenage literacy in urban areas.

Dina Merrill

Without love, we ~~are~~ nothing —
With love, we ~~can~~ accomplish
miracles!

In the most horrific experiences of humankind, love not only endures, it thrives.

As the executive director of AIDS Action, Daniel Zingale stands in the front lines of the war against the AIDS epidemic. AIDS Action is an AIDS advocacy organization dedicated to defeating the life-threatening illness and improving the quality of life for hundreds of thousands of HIV-infected Americans. As political director of the Human Rights Campaign, the nation's largest gay and lesbian political rights organization, Zingale has proven himself to be one of the movement's best political strategists. Before joining the HRC, Zingale attended the University of California at Berkeley's undergraduate program as well as Harvard University's John F. Kennedy School of Government, where he earned a Master's in Public Administration. Zingale has also served as managing director of government relations for the American Psychological Association and as the state of California's deputy controller.

until it's over
AIDS **ACTION**

In the most horrific
experiences of
humankind, love not
only endures,
it thrives.
Daniel Zingale

I try to act in accord with the Buddhist precept of increasing the happiness and decreasing the suffering of all living creatures.

A rlene Blum believes her passion for mountain climbing to be a powerful metaphor for achieving any demanding goal: to get to the top, one must commit physically, intellectually, and psychologically. Blum has demonstrated this vision in the more than fifteen mountaineering expeditions that she has led. She has climbed extensively in the Himalayas, and she led the first American climb of Annapurna, a peak measuring 26,500 feet, recorded in the book *Annapurna: A Woman's Place*. In addition, she has climbed Mount Everest and Mount McKinley. Blum's lectures on leadership training and personal potential can be accessed on-line via her website www.arleneblum.com. Blum has a doctorate in biophysical chemistry, and she has taught at several universities. Her research has been instrumental in banning tris, a cancer-causing chemical that was used as a flame retardant in children's sleepwear. It is no surprise that she received a Gold Medal from the Society of Women Geographers, joining such heroines as Amelia Earhart and Margaret Mead.

Arlene Blum
LECTURES

I try to act in accord with
the Buddhist precept of increasing
the happiness & decreasing the
suffering of all living creatures

Arlene Blum

Love is giving of one's self, and trusting in the other person, but the most important thing I know about love is how I feel toward my wife, Elaine. She is everything in the world to me. I'd give my life for her. To me that's true love.

Back in the days when doctors thought that lifting weights brought on heart attacks, Jack LaLanne was preaching the novel concepts of exercise and a healthy diet. At the age of fifteen, after hearing a pioneer nutritionist speak, he began an exercise and diet regimen that he has maintained for sixty years. At twenty-one, he opened the nation's first modern health studio, forty years before gyms became fashionable. In the 1950s, he began the first nationally syndicated television show on exercise and nutrition. LaLanne was the first to encourage all people, including those with disabilities, to reap the benefits of exercise through his TV programs and his long list of book titles. At eighty-four, LaLanne looks younger every day.

From the desk of **Jack LaLanne**

Love is giving of one's self,
and trusting in the other person,
but the most important thing I
know about love is how I feel
toward my wife, Elaine. She is
everything in the world to me.
I'd give my life for her. To me
that's true love.

Love & exercise
Jack LaLanne

The most important thing I know about living on earth is love, espeically love for persons with mental retardation.

Will you love the special child, the child with mental retardation? When your own child follows your example you will experience love three times. The love you give the special child, the love he/she will give back to you and to your daughter or son. Thus you and your children will be closer to the Lord because of the love you have showered on His special children whom He has created and put together with you and all of humanity here on earth.

A s executive vice president of the Joseph P. Kennedy, Jr. Foundation and Honorary Chairman of Special Olympics International, Eunice Kennedy Shriver has for more than three decades been a leader in the worldwide struggle to improve the lives of individuals with mental retardation. Born in Brookline, Massachusetts, the fifth of nine children of Joseph P. and Rose Fitzgerald Kennedy, Eunice Mary Kennedy received a bachelor of science degree in sociology from Stanford University. Following graduation, she worked for the State Department, and the Penitentiary for Women in Alderson, West Virginia, the House of the Good Shepherd in Chicago, and the Chicago juvenile court. In 1957, Mrs. Shriver took over the direction of the Joseph P. Kennedy, Jr. Foundation. The foundation was established in 1946 as a memorial to Joseph P. Kennedy Jr., the eldest son, who was killed in World War II. Mrs. Shriver has received many honors and awards, including the Presidential Medal of Freedom, the Legion of Honor, and the Laetare Medal of the University of Notre Dame.

The most important thing
I know about living
on earth is love
especially love for persons
with mental Retardation.

Will you love the
special child, the child
with mental Retardation?
When your own child
follows your example you
will experiance love
three times

Eunice Kennedy Shriver is married to Sargent Shriver and has five children: Robert Sargent Shriver III, Maria Owings Shriver Schwarzenegger, Timothy Perry Shriver, Mark Kennedy Shriver, and Anthony Paul Kennedy Shriver.

The love you give the
special child, the love
he/she will give back
to you and to your
daughter or son. Thus
you and your children
will be closer to the
Lord because of the
love you have showered
on his special children
whom He has created
and put together with
you and all of humanity
here on Earth

**The most important thing I know about living is love.
Nothing surpasses the benefits received by a human being
who makes compassion and love the objective of his or her
life. For it is only by compassion and love that anyone
fulfills successfully their own life's journey. Nothing equals
love. Only God surpasses it, a power which He demonstrated by His life on earth and by His loving commitment
to each one of us, and to all of us, whom He has created
and put together here on His earth.**

Sargent Shriver has made a lifetime career out of public service,
acting always for the benefit of others. After graduating from
Yale University and Yale Law School, Shriver served in the U.S.
Navy for five years. After joining the staff of Ambassador Joseph P.
Kennedy, he had the opportunity to participate in forming some of
the programs developed by the Joseph P. Kennedy, Jr. Foundation.
Among his many achievements, Shriver has served as the president
of the Chicago Board of Education, been the organizer and the first
director of the Peace Corps, created a wealth of social programs,
and served as U.S. Ambassador to France. In 1970, he was named a
partner, specializing in international law and foreign affairs, in the
law firm of Fried, Frank, Harris, Shriver and Jacobson. Shriver
received the Democratic nomination for vice president in 1972,
with George McGovern in the presidential slot. In 1984, Shriver
was appointed president of the Special Olympics, and he directed
the operation and international development of sports programs in
countries worldwide. Shriver assumed the position of chairman of
the board of Special Olympics in 1990, and he has worked tirelessly
on behalf of the organization.

The most important thing I know about living is love. Nothing surpasses the benefits received by a human being who makes compassion and love the objective of his or her life. For it is only by compassion and love that anyone fulfills successfully their own life's journey. Nothing equals love. Only God surpasses it, a power which He demonstrated by His life on earth and by His loving commitment to each one of us, and to all of us, whom He has created & put together here on His earth.

Sargent Shriver

Love is the only force that is completely without limit, condition, or barrier. So, it is forever—a total yes to another in the promise: "I love you."

Tim Shriver is president and CEO of Special Olympics International. In that capacity, he serves over one million Special Olympics athletes and their families in 145 countries worldwide. Prior to joining Special Olympics, Shriver launched and supervised New Haven, Connecticut's Public Schools' Social Development Project, the country's most noted school-based project focused on preventing substance abuse, violence, dropout, and teen pregnancy. Prior to starting the project, Shriver was a teacher in the New Haven public schools and a teacher and counselor in the University of Connecticut's Upward Bound program. In 1994, Shriver helped launch and currently chairs the Collaborative for the Advancement of Social and Emotional Learning (CASEL) at the University of Illinois, a national organization to promote effective school-based prevention programming. In recent years, he has applied his educational interests to film. He was the co-producer of DreamWorks studios' 1997 release *Amistad*. Shriver received his undergraduate education at Yale University, a master's degree in religion and education from Catholic University, and a doctorate in education from the University of Connecticut. He chairs the National Advisory Board of the Shriver Center at the University of Maryland at Baltimore, and he serves on the Boards of the J. F. K. Library Foundation, American Bar Association Commission on Disability, Amistad America, Inc., and the Education Compact for Learning and Citizenship. He and his wife, Linda Potter, reside in the Washington, D.C., area with their five children.

Timothy Shriver

Love is the only force that is completely without limit, condition, or barrier. So, it is forever - a total yes to another in the promise -

"I LOVE YOU"

Special Olympics, Inc.

Timothy Shriver

Love of life and all living things is the most precious love of all.

I n 1979, while commuting to the University of Arkansas to complete her graduate studies, Wilma Mankiller suffered a near-fatal head-on automobile accident. In an effort to recover from the injuries she sustained, she adopted the Cherokee tradition of "being of good mind." This tradition—the ability to think positively and transform situations into better paths—has been the backbone of her leadership abilities. In the historic tribal election of 1987, the members of the Cherokee Nation of Oklahoma elected Mankiller as their Principal Chief; she was the first woman to assume such a position. Mankiller was born and raised in the rural community of Rocky Mountain in Adair County, Oklahoma. At age eleven, her family moved to California as part of the Bureau of Indian Affairs Relocation Program. After the demonstration by American Indian activists at Alcatraz in 1969, she felt a call to action. By 1974, she and her two children had moved back to Oklahoma, where they now live. When she left office in 1995, Mankiller coauthored *Mankiller: A Chief and Her People.* Throughout her career Wilma Mankiller has been honored with countless awards, among them the National Women's Hall of Fame in 1993, the Humanitarian Award from the National Conference of Christians and Jews, *Who's Who in America*, one of the Fifty Most Important People in the United States in 1996, and the Presidential Medal of Freedom in 1998.

WILMA MANKILLER

*Love of life and all living
things is the most precious
love of all.*

*Wa— Mankiller
August 3, 1999*

The most important thing I know about love is . . . it is the most peaceful, confusing, safe, craziest, appealing constant emotion we have. If I only had one feeling to feel, I would want to feel love and loved. Love is to share, to have and to keep honestly. Above all, I know love comes from God, whatever we believe!

I n 1984, Mother Love resigned from her job as a bus driver with one eloquently simple letter, "I am leaving to become a star." Her premonition proved true; not long after, while attending a bridal shower in search of her own wedding dress, she did an ad-lib comedy routine that won her a slot on Cleveland's local radio station. Since that time, Mother Love has distinguished herself as an author, an actress, and a comedic radio personality. Now with *Forgive or Forget*, her new daytime talk show, every day is Mother's Day. Love believes that by referring to her own tough experiences, she can help people come to terms with their problems. After growing up in the Cleveland projects, she left college to go on welfare when she became a mother. Throughout all this, she has maintained drive and focus, but it is her special insight into love that helps people on her show.

FORGIVE OR FORGET

The most important thing I know about Love is... It is the most peaceful, confusing safe, craziest, appalling constant emotion we have. If I only had one feeling to feel, I would want to feel love and loved. Love is to share, to have and to keep honestly. Above all I know Love comes from Gods whatever we believe! Mother Love

Mother Love

Love is the willingness to accept another person with all of his or her faults and limitations, and to be infinitely grateful that this other person accepts you with all of yours.

In 1981, Rabbi Harold S. Kushner brought the American public a new way to understand life's tragic dimensions with his bestseller *When Bad Things Happen to Good People*. Since that time, it has been translated into twelve languages. Kushner is the Rabbi Laureate of Temple Israel in Natick, Massachusetts. He is considered to be a dynamic speaker, with a strong reputation for his thought-provoking topics; he has moved millions with his lectures and seminars. In 1995, Kushner was awarded the Christopher Medal for his book *When All You've Ever Wanted Isn't Enough*. Rabbi Kushner graduated from Columbia University, was ordained by the Jewish Theological Seminary in 1960, and was awarded a doctoral degree there in 1972. He has been granted six honorary doctorates, and he has completed studies at the Hebrew University in Jerusalem and the Harvard Divinity School.

from the desk of
Rabbi Harold S. Kushner

Love is the willingness to
accept another person with all of
his or her faults and limitations,
and to be infinitely grateful that
this other person accepts you with
all of yours.

Harold Kushner

Love is letting go of fear. Only through total trust and freedom from possessing can love thrive.

As a child, Dorothy Ann Willlis's parents taught her that the only two things of real value in life were family and hard work. As an adult, Ann Richards took these words to heart. After completing her Bachelor of Arts degree at Baylor University in 1954, she did additional course work at the University of Texas in Austin. It was there that she fell in love with politics, a passion she remained dedicated to, even while her four children were young. In 1976, Richards was first elected to public office, taking a seat on the Travis County Commissioners Court. Six years later, when she was elected State Treasurer, she became the first woman to assume a statewide public office in Texas in fifty years. After two terms, Richards was elected Governor of Texas in 1990. Her administration was particularly active in issues of education, public safety, efficiency, and economic development. After a successful term as governor, Richards became a senior advisor with Verner, Liipfert, Bernhard, McPherson & Hand, a Washington-based law firm. In addition to serving on several prominent boards, she devotes her time to her family, including seven beautiful grandchildren.

Love is letting go of fear. Only through total trust and freedom from posessing can love thrive.

Ann Richards

Education is founded in love and respect. The pursuit of technology provides access to data and even job security. Education can reinforce and provide strong family values and high moral standards when schools and communities have the courage to base priorities on the country's greatest asset—its children.

Charles MacLaughlin is the director of Quincy High School's Heritage Program in Quincy, Massachusetts. Mr. Mac, as his students call him, designs alternate learning curricula in order to benefit students whose needs are not being met in the regular classroom. Recently, he made headlines for working with Lauralee Summer to create a school strategy more suited to her interests and her intellect. After hearing that she was patient with children and she loved to read, he suggested that she teach reading to younger children. This plan helped her to move from barely passing to winning acceptance to one of the most prestigious schools in the country, Harvard University.

QUINCY PUBLIC SCHOOLS   Quincy, Massachusetts

EUGENE W. CREEDON, Superintendent

Where excellence is the tradition

THE HERITAGE PROGRAM
Quincy High School

Charles MacLaughlin, Director

8/5/99

Education is founded in love and respect.
The pursuit of Technology provides access
to data and even job security. Education
can reinforce and provide strong family
values and high moral standards when
schools and communities have the courage
to base priorities on the country's
greatest asset — its children

Charles MacLaughlin

Love is the thread we hold on tightly to keep us from crossing over to death and it is the strong thread of God's love that guides us out of death and into His love. Without love, I would be a water balloon of tears, shapeless and expanding in every direction. Without the care and faithfulness of my loved ones, I would have nothing to hold me in place, nothing to keep me from spilling into the wide and deep infinity of the exterior world. Love pushes me into shape from all sides, it holds me like a glass holds water, and when I am truly loved, I am as clear as the clearest water. Love is unconditional—or it isn't love. We don't love because we understand another person; we love because we can't help the loving. We love other people because of their affinity to and difference from us; we love them because of their humanity and because of their pain.

By the time she was nine years old, Lauralee Summer had moved eight times to three states. She spent her youth rotating through homeless shelters, finding her strength and her hope from her mother's creativity. After living with an aunt for a while, her mother decided to move them to Boston, in pursuit of cultural and educational influences. There, Lauralee lived in a foster home while her mother saved money and got an apartment. As she began ninth grade, she returned to her mother's house and attended Quincy High School. An amazing teacher, Mr. MacLaughlin, helped her to design her own unique curriculum. With his support and her amazing drive, Lauralee excelled academically, athletically, and personally. In the spring of 1998, she graduated from Harvard University with a degree in children's studies.

Love is the thread we hold on tightly to keep us from crossing over to death and it is the strong thread of God's love that guides us out of death and into His love. Without love, I would be a water balloon of tears, shapeless and expanding in every direction. Without the care and faithfulness of my loved ones, I would have nothing to hold me in place, nothing to keep me from spilling into the wide and deep infinity of the exterior world. Love pushes me into shape from all sides, it holds me like a glass holds water, and when I am truly loved I am as clear as the clearest water. *Love* is unconditional, or it isn't love. We don't love because we understand another person, we love because we can't help the loving. We love other people because of their affinity to and difference from us; we love them because of their humanity and because of their pain. *Lauralee Summer*

"Love is like the lion's tooth." WBY

A s a kid, Robert Pinsky's imagination was first captured by the way the train conductor's words sounded, as the conductor cried, "Passengers going to Hoboken, change trains at Summit." Born in 1940 in Long Branch, New Jersey, he went on to earn a bachelor's degree from Rutgers University, and then earned a prestigious fellowship to Stanford University in support of his master's and doctoral work in English. He received a National Endowment for the Humanities Fellowship in 1974, and in 1975 published his collection of poems *Sadness and Happiness*. Other poetry collections followed: *An Explanation of America* in 1980, which won the Saxifrage Prize; *History of My Heart* in 1984, awarded the William Carlos Williams award of the Poetry Society of America; *The Want Bone* in 1990; and *The Figured Wheel: New and Collected Poems 1966–1996*, which was nominated for the Pulitzer Prize in Poetry. Professor Pinsky is also known for his translation work, most notably *The Inferno of Dante* (1994), which won the Los Angeles Times Book Award in poetry. In 1997, Pinsky was named the thirty-ninth poet laureate of the United States. In addition to a long career in teaching, currently at Boston University teaching graduate writing, he is the poetry editor of the on-line magazine *Slate* and the editor of a collection of love poems called *The Handbook of Heartache* (1998).

ROBERT PINSKY

" *Love is like the lion's tooth.* "

W B Y

Love is . . . finding your soulmate! . . . without losing your soul . . . !

Marty Ingels's marriage to Shirley Jones was a showbiz fusion. At seventeen, Rodgers and Hammerstein scouted Jones while auditioning for a chorus role in *South Pacific*. She went on to become America's sweetheart with roles in numerous films and television shows, including Mrs. Partridge in *The Partridge Family*. Ingels first received national visibility in the sitcom *I'm Dickens, He's Fenster* with John Austin in 1963. Since then, he has continued in television, film, and numerous commercial roles. Currently, Marty and Shirley enjoy appearing together on television talk shows and in seasonal productions of *Love Letters*. They live in Beverly Hills.

Love is...
Finding your soulmate!
Shirley & Marty
(...without losing your Soul...)
SECURITY
Shirley
INSECURITY

Love is accepting one's right to be themselves without judgment!

Sarah M. Greene has been chief executive officer of the National Head Start Association (NHSA) since 1991. NHSA is dedicated to meeting the concerns of the Head Start community, and represents over 800,000 children in 2,196 Head Start programs nationwide. Acting as ambassador for the Head Start community and providing insight for the future direction of Head Start, Ms. Greene has recently taken her organization to an international level. She served as delegation leader, with Head Start delegates from across the United States, in educational exchange programs to Australia, Zimbabwe, South Africa, and China. Ms. Greene's experience in Head Start began as a teacher at a Florida-based program. She quickly moved through the ranks to become the director of the program, then assumed the role of executive director of both the Community Action Agency and Head Start Program. Currently, Greene serves on a number of boards and advisory panels, including the National Health and Education Consortium and "Free to Grow," a project funded by the Robert Wood Johnson Foundation. She is co-editor of *Head Start Works*, published in 1995. A native of Florida, Greene received a Bachelor of Arts in English at Bethune Cookman College in Daytona Beach, Florida, and a master's degree in administration and supervision from Nova University in Ft. Lauderdale, Florida.

**National
Head Start
Association**

Love is accepting one's right to
be themselves without judgement!

Sarah M. Greene
CEO, NHSA

Treating people, not as "its"—objects to be exploited for our own selfish purposes—but as "thous"—human beings created in God's image and embodying His holy presence in the world—is the key to heaven and to loving our neighbor as ourselves.

In 1980, when a Christian clergyman declared that God did not hear the prayers of Jews, it was Rabbi Yechiel Z. Eckstein who reached out to successfully initiate a dialogue with him. During his years as a prominent Jewish leader, Rabbi Eckstein built powerful bridges between the Jewish community and evangelical Christians. Born and raised in Ottawa, Canada, Rabbi Eckstein received a master's degree from Yeshiva University in 1975 and a second from Columbia University and Union Theological Seminary in 1997. He served for six years as co-director of interreligious affairs for the Anti-Defamation League, where he received acclaim for developing the nation's first Holocaust curriculum for the Chicago public schools. Eckstein has authored five books and appeared on numerous television and radio shows in support of building communications between Jews and Christians. He currently hosts *On Wings of Eagles* specials on radio and television. Eckstein lives with his wife, Bonnie, and their three daughters in the Chicago area.

INTERNATIONAL FELLOWSHIP OF CHRISTIANS AND JEWS

RABBI YECHIEL ECKSTEIN
Founder and President

Treating people, not as "its" — objects to be exploited for our own selfish purposes — but as "thous" — human beings created in God's image and embodying His holy presence in the world — is the key to heaven and to loving our neighbor as ourselves.

Yechiel Eckstein

Do not judge strangers harshly. Remember that every stranger you meet is you.

S idney Sheldon arrived on Hollywood's back doorstep as a teenager in 1937. There he worked as a script reader for only $25 a week. Less than a decade later, after a brief time in the air force, Sheldon wrote three musicals, which played simultaneously on Broadway. The Chicago boy had found success, and it followed in everything he wrote—from musicals to movies to novels. In 1948, he was awarded an Academy Award for best original screenplay, followed by Screen Writers Guild Awards for best musical for two years running. Upon a return to Broadway writing, he was awarded a Tony in the 1950s. During the early 1960s, he moved to television, writing and producing *The Patty Duke Show* and *I Dream of Jeannie*. In 1969, Sheldon published his first novel, *The Naked Face*, a mystery, which immediately won numerous awards. Since then, he has sold more than 280 million copies of his sixteen novels, and *The Guinness Book of World Records* refers to him as "the Most Translated Author in the World."

Sidney Sheldon

Do not judge
strangers harshly.
Remember that
every stranger you
meet is you.

Sidney Sheldon

You can only love others to the extent that you can love yourself.

r. Weil stands at the intersection of traditional Western medicine and alternative therapies. Born in Philadelphia in 1942, Weil received his A.B. degree as well as his M.D. from Harvard University, graduating in 1968. He published his first book, *The Natural Mind*, following a year with the National Institute of Mental Health. After several years of traveling in North and South America and in Africa, collecting information on medicines in other cultures, he served on the research staff of the Harvard Botanical Museum. Currently, Weil is director of the Program in Integrative Medicine of the College of Medicine, University of Arizona; it attempts to include alternative therapies in the instruction of traditional medicine. He is the founder of the Foundation for Integrative Medicine in Tucson, and editor-in-chief of the journal *Integrative Medicine*. Andrew Weil is the author of seven widely read books, which include *Eight Weeks to Optimum Health* and *Spontaneous Healing*.

ANDREW WEIL, MD

YOU CAN ONLY LOVE
OTHERS TO THE EXTENT
THAT YOU CAN LOVE
YOURSELF.

Love seems like a feeling, but really it is the sole condition of our existence.

Jane Smiley was awarded a Pulitzer Prize as well as several other awards for her examination of Midwestern life in *A Thousand Acres*. She made the international bestseller list with *Moo*, a satirical examination of academia. In her latest work, *The All-True Travels and Adventures of Lidie Newton*, Smiley sets her story against the background of the moral and political conflicts of the Civil War, and a young woman's coming of age. She was born in Los Angeles, and spent her childhood in St. Louis. She earned her undergraduate degree at Vassar College and her doctorate at the University of Iowa. Smiley has authored additional works, including *The Age of Grief, The Greenlanders,* and *Ordinary Love and Good Will.*

Love seems like a feeling, but
really it is the sole condition
of our existence.

Jane Smiley

The most important thing I know about love is: it is at its very best when it is mutual!

In 1956, Pauline Friedman Phillips, a thirty-seven-year-old house-wife and mother of two teenagers, called the *San Francisco Chronicle* and made the convincing argument that she could write a better advice column than their current one. Though they were originally unimpressed with her lack of experience, she won them over with her claim that she was an "amateur wailing wall without a portfolio." Within two months, she was the author of a nationally syndicated column, and her large reading audience has supported her faithfully for over forty years. She is well known for projects such as the 1985 Operation Dear Abby, where she invited readers to send letters to American servicemen and women overseas, prompting the start of many friendships. She advocates for the mentally ill and the physically disabled and is the founding director of the National Foundation for AIDS Research. Through all of this, she turns out her column 365 days each year.

Dear Abby

The most important thing I know about love is: it is at its very best when it is mutual!

Abigail Van Buren

I can see a better world because it exists today in small pockets of this country and in a small pocket of every person's heart.

Rosa Parks, often called the mother of the modern day civil rights movement, is world renowned for her courageous actions on December 1, 1955, when she refused to give up her seat on a segregated bus to a white male passenger. Her arrest led to the Montgomery bus boycott, a 381-day demonstration that marked the beginning of the end of segregation in America, and brought the Reverend Martin Luther King Jr. into the public eye. Of course, Rosa and her husband, Raymond, were committed to fighting peacefully for civil and human rights long before this event; together, they encouraged others to vote, pool financial resources, and advocate for quality formal education. Throughout her life, Rosa has shown a steadfast commitment to community development, especially by remaining active with youth in the NAACP. The Rosa and Raymond Parks Institute for Self Development, based in Detroit, is the organization she cofounded in 1987, in honor of her husband, Raymond (1903–1977). The institute helps youth reach their highest potential, using Mrs. Parks's philosophy of "quiet strength." Among her numerous awards, Mrs. Parks received the Presidential Medal of Freedom in 1996, the nation's highest civilian honor. On February 4, 1999, Representative Julia Carson of Indiana introduced H.R. Bill 573, which was signed into law May 3, 1999, by President Clinton. It made Rosa Parks the 250th person to receive the Congressional Gold Medal of Honor from the United States of America.

Rosa & Raymond Parks Institute for Self Development

I can see a better world because it exists today in small pockets of this country and in a small pocket of every person's heart.

Rosa L. Parks

9 - 2 - 99